Big Buds

Growers guide to get the biggest yields from your plants

By Jay Cheeba

☐ **Copyright 2016 by Jay Cheeba - All rights reserved.**

This document is geared towards providing exact and reliable information in regards to the topic and issue covered. The publication is sold with the idea that the publisher is not required to render accounting, officially permitted, or otherwise, qualified services. If advice is necessary, legal or professional, a practiced individual in the profession should be ordered.

- From a Declaration of Principles which was accepted and approved equally by a Committee of the American Bar Association and a Committee of Publishers and Associations.

In no way is it legal to reproduce, duplicate, or transmit any part of this document in either electronic means or in printed format. Recording of this publication is strictly prohibited and any storage of this document is not allowed unless with written permission from the publisher. All rights reserved.

The information provided herein is stated to be truthful and consistent, in that any liability, in terms of inattention or otherwise, by any usage or abuse of any policies, processes, or directions contained within is the solitary and utter responsibility of the recipient reader. Under no circumstances will any legal responsibility or blame be held against the publisher for any reparation, damages, or monetary loss due to the information herein, either directly or indirectly.

Respective authors own all copyrights not held by the publisher.

The information herein is offered for informational purposes solely, and is universal as so. The presentation of the information is without contract or any type of guarantee assurance.

The trademarks that are used are without any consent, and the publication of the trademark is without permission or backing by the trademark owner. All trademarks and brands within this book are for clarifying purposes only and are the owned by the owners themselves, not affiliated with this document.

Table of Contents

Introduction 4

Chapter 1: Increase Light Sensitivity 12

Chapter 2: Manipulating Plant Structure 17

Chapter 3: Using Nutrients 27

Chapter 4: Temperature and Humidity Control 45

Chapter 5: Drying and Curing Buds 51

Chapter 6: Timing the Harvest 58

Conclusion 67

Introduction

Growing marijuana indoor has seen a dramatic rise in popularity in recent years due to legalization in US and other countries. When it is cultivated properly, it produces good quality weed that is much better than the stuff that is sold on the streets. Indoor growing involves use of artificial light that is used as a replacement for sunlight. Growers have been known to employ hydroponics to grow marijuana indoor to great effect as well. Growing marijuana hydroponically indicates the use of water, nutrients and air instead of using soil. Since hydroponic system makes it easier for the roots to absorb the nutrients by bypassing the web of roots, it helps in faster growth of the plant. Some growers are also known to germinate seeds – which is a process of getting the seeds to sprout.

There are two basic advantages that growing marijuana indoors has over growing marijuana outdoors: security and space. When grown outdoors there is a threat of theft, torrential downpour or pest infestation and one also needs a substantial amount of space so it will be practically impossible for city dwellers to grow it. Also, unless one lives near the Equator, there will only be one harvest a year compared to growing indoors which can produce perpetual harvests. Growing marijuana is easy because it is a strong and fast growing plant and it can be discreetly done. It generally takes approximately 6 months for the plant to go from seed stage to a stage where it can be smoked.

Genetics

The building block to achieving potent buds and optimum yields is the genetics of the plant. The genetics of the plants defines how the plant grows, how the bud fattens and how much yield it produces. The strains that are available in the market today offer much greater yields than the ones that were available just a decade ago. The potency of the strain, how easy it is to grow and yields it produces have increased steadily over the decade and growers are experimenting on new strains and improving the old favorites all around the world.

Before following the steps that involve increasing the yield from the marijuana plant, it is very important that a grower starts with selecting high yielding strains. Investing on a high yielding strain is one of the most important aspect of increasing yields from the grow space. Listed below are three proven high-yielding strains that can be purchase online safely and legally:

Tangerine Dream

This strain by Barney's Farm in Amsterdam is remarkably strong and is special because of its smell and look. It looks like no other marijuana strain and offers a tangy citrus aroma and flavor. It is also a strain that produces great yields.

1. **Aurora Indica**

This strain is perfect for stealth growers who look for a high yielding plant which harvests quickly. It actually

also stays short and bushy; which makes growing them much easier. They require low nutrients than other strains and have a sedating effect. It also has an almost minty tone to its smell.

2. Wonder Woman

This is one of the highest yielding strains and is easy to grow. It responds well to Low Stress Training (LST) and other training methods. It seems to behave well with relatively high level of nutrients but makes up for that by producing great yields with long, dense buds. It grows to a good size – not too tall and not too short and has a relaxing mental effect.

Earlier, a veteran marijuana grower would be required to let someone in on the secrets to learn the art of growing marijuana, but today, anyone with the will and an internet access can grow marijuana. There are numerous articles and books available online to teach anybody the basics of growing weed indoors. Most of these books point to using seed banks or clones from a local grower. It is very tough to get high quality buds if one uses mid-grade seeds or clones. Investing in top shelf genetics will produce top shelf buds. There are various methods of increasing the tarpene levels in your plant so that it tastes and smells better. Tarpene is a chemical that is present in household spices as well like cinnamon and cloves and gives the buds its smell and taste. A good airflow and sufficient ventilation is very important to allow your plant to flower properly. Even after all these steps, what a marijuana grower wants is to produce better yields. Almost every marijuana grower wants to increase their yield without the added investment of time and money.

This book will help illustrate the process to increase the yield from the same growing space. There are 5 basics steps that constitute this process:

1. **Increase light sensitivity**

   It can be generally considered a thumb rule that the most effective way to increase bud size at the time of flowering is to increase the light intensity. But there is a risk of causing light burns on your buds by increasing the intensity of the grow lights too much. There is however another way to increase the sensitivity of the plant to light.

2. **Manipulating plant structure**
   Training the plant to grow bigger and wider so that the buds grow evenly over the space will lead to greater yields.

3. **Using nutrients**
   There is no doubt that every grower knows the marijuana plant needs nutrients to grow but using the right nutrients in the perfect amount is necessary to get better yields from the plant.

4. **Temperature and Humidity control**
   It is imperative that the marijuana grows in a good environment for it to produce potent yields. Learning to read signs that point to stress in the plant is very important so that the heat and humidity of the grow room can be altered accordingly.

5. **Timing the harvest**
   Generally, all strains of marijuana have a 14-21 day window during which the buds can be harvested.

But it is important to time it correctly to make sure that the buds have ripened fully before harvest.

Chapter 1: Increase Light Sensitivity

A lot of growers are usually perplexed when talking about the ways to increase the number of buds they are producing and also the size and density. The simplest solution, most often, is to increase the light intensity. If there is nothing wrong with the health of the plant and there aren't any other major problems with the plant or the soil, it is usually the poor lighting of the grow room that is to blame for poor yields.

If the lighting is not appropriate in the vegetative state, the plant will tend to reach towards the light which will result in the plants having a lot of stem between its nodes and leaves. Enough light intensity needs to be provided for preventing the plants from stretching or growing so tall that it falls over. Tall plants are harder to provide light coverage for during the flowering stage and hence they will result in poor yields in most indoor setups. Higher light intensity drives the growth and production of buds.

Once the cannabis plant starts producing buds, anything that can be done to increase the intensity of light will go a long way to increase the yields. Marijuana grow lights are widely available and they provide the optimum light levels that the plant needs to grow. It is tough to provide adequate intensity of light to all the plants if they are too tall or growing in an uneven manner. That is why it is very important to provide high intensity light to the plants when they are in a vegetative stage.

After the plant has reached the flowering stage, there is very little that can be done for the height of the plants without risking hurting them. The best thing to do at that point is to increase the intensity of the light as much as possible. It should also be kept in mind that too intense light or too high temperature is also a deterrent to the actual produce as they burn off terpenoids (that control smell and taste) and cannabinoids (that control potency) and in the process lowers the quality of the buds. Best results come when the plant from its infant stage is given a steady intense light source that will make the plants grow steadily and also cause the buds to swell in the flowering stage. Even in the wild, where a marijuana bud which gets pollinated by the wind and air, the plant refrains from putting too much effort on the hidden middle and lower buds and only the buds that are at the top and have good exposure tend to grow fat.

It is unlikely that an indoor grower will provide too much light to their marijuana plants as the marijuana plants can consume a surprising amount of light naturally. So, as long as the grower keeps the light at an appropriate distance, chances of hurting the plant are less.

The various kinds of lights used by the growers normally are:

1. **CFLs and other fluorescent grow lights** can be kept as close to the marijuana plant as possible as they are relatively weak in intensity. They are best for growing in tight spaces and are especially favorable for stealth farming. But if there is a need to increase the intensity of the light, more CFLs need to be bought as there is no scope of bringing the CFL closer to the plant for increasing intensity. Other types of fluorescent lighting also use a similar technology to CFLs but are available in different shapes.

2. **LED grow lights** generally should be kept at a distance of least of 12", and 3W/5W models should be kept at a distance greater than 18". Modern grow lights are very powerful and can burn a plant easily. So, it is advisable to read the manufacturer's instructions when deciding how close they should be kept.

3. **HID Grow Lights (Metal Halide/High Pressure Sodium lights)** should be kept at least 1 to 2 feet away from the plant. The size of the bulb also determines if the light should be closer or farther away. A seasoned grower will always suggest a new grower to start with CFLs instead of HID because they overestimate the amount of heat that is being produced by the HID. But it is important to note that a 250W CFL will essentially produce the same amount of heat as a 250W HID, but the HID will be much brighter and will help in increasing the yields. Also, unlike CFLs HIDs come fitted with an exhaust system to accommodate cooling.

No matter which grow light is used, it is absolutely necessary to have some sort of cooling or exhaust system in place to prevent heat stress and bring in more fresh air for the plants. There is another aspect of increasing yield when talking about light intensity - the sensitivity of the plant. If light is considered as food for the plant, using too much light would be equivalent to over-eating.

Using too much light will lead to light burn, even if the temperature of the grow space is cool. But if the plants metabolism can be increased, it will enable the plant to consume much more light and increase the yield. One method of doing that is increasing the level of CO_2 in the grow room during the flowering stage. How increasing CO_2 levels works is that it increases the ability of the plant to use more light at higher levels. It is to be understood that CO_2 is not a way to compensate for weak lighting but actually a way for the plant to use more light than it possible can without being burnt.

It takes a lot of light for the plant to hit its saturation level, so unless a 1000W grow light is being used, the plant is already able to use all the light they're receiving. To summarize – adding CO_2 does not increase yields directly, but increases the amount of energy that a plant can produce under high intensity lights. If the plant is already consuming as much light as possible, increasing the flow of CO_2 will not help in increasing the yields. Since CO_2 is harmful to humans, it is also advisable to seal off the grow area when increasing the flow of CO_2.

Chapter 2: Manipulating Plant Structure

One of the most inexpensive ways of increasing yields from the marijuana plants in your grow space is manipulating the plants because it does not require the grower to change anything in the setup and does not involved purchase of expensive grow lights or nutrients. Manipulating a plant that does not involve cutting it is referred to as **Low Stress Training or LST**. The idea behind LST is to force the plant to not grow tall and thin but grow short, flat and wide.

Photo Courtesy: growweedeasy.com

The plant in the picture above looks short when viewed from the side but from the top it shows how big a surface area it is providing for the plant to absorb the light. They act like solar panels which continually soak up the light from the grow lights. The flat top allows for a good distribution of light emanating from the grow light and ensures that more of the plant gets exposed to the light. Attempting to experiment with LST should almost always start when the plant is very young, as this type of shape is extremely hard to achieve when the plant has grown into a tall triangle shape with a tall main bud. Another variety of LST is when a grower uses a screen or net, which forces the plant to grow in a flat shape at the top. This process is called **"Screen of Green" or SCROG** in short. An example of plants using the SCROG methodology is in the picture below:

Photo Courtesy: growweedeasy.com

It can be noted from the picture that the plants are getting exposed to the light in a direct way. This direct light will enable the plant to grow bigger buds and increase the yield from the plant. However, to use SCROG one needs to invest in a screen and take out time during the vegetative state to train the plant to grow along the screen.

Photo Courtesy: growweedeasy.com

Another popular training method for plants to increase their yield is called "**Supercropping**" – as shown in the picture above. It means that the stem of the plant is broken very carefully to ensure that the skin does not crack, but the stem lays flat and grows horizontally. Supercropping can be used in conjunction with another method like LST or SCROG to get better results in terms of yield or it can be used as a standalone method. Anytime a bud seems to grow out of proportion or taller than others, supercropping can be used to force the plant to bend.

There are also methods when talking about plant training that involves actually cutting the plant or modifying the stem or leaves in some way. There are basically two options to do that: **to "top" the plant and to "FIM" the plant**. Both the options involve removing some of the growth from the main bud of the young marijuana plant, which cause the plant to stop focusing on one bud and instead create many buds. The image below can show how plant growth patterns change because of topping or FIMing from a very young age.

Photo Courtesy: growweedeasy.com

There is another method of training a plant, which is extremely dangerous for the plant and as such, a matter of

23

much debate and controversy among the growers. It is known as **defoliation**. It has been recommended that growers first set their hands and have a few successful grows using the earlier mentioned techniques before trying this method as this can hurt or even kill the plants if not done correctly. Defoliation is an extreme form of marijuana growth control. It is a controversial subject among expert growers and both sides of the argument have defended their position vehemently over the years.

Growers who oppose the idea of defoliation do so with the argument that the practice of defoliation involves cutting off the leaves of the plant which can never lead to better yield. Supporters of the technique say that it is more important that we understand how the plant grows instead of assuming how it grows or how people think it grows. Misguided defoliation will obviously end up killing the plant, but when done properly there is evidence to suggest that it indeed will lead to better yields. Defoliation is known to increase yield in other crops like cowpeas – which is an example often cited by the supporters of this technique.

In defoliation, when the plant starts growing, the leaves are not allowed to stay on the plant for more than two-three weeks. It is advisable to start at the top to reduce shading. Removing the lower leaves usually contributes nothing to the objective of exposing shaded out mid and low level leaves. But some people do it anyway to ensure uniformity. Some growers resort to intensive defoliation with a version of supercropping (twist and train) using a basic net for support. This is why the process is termed as "controversial" because some growers think that impeding the natural growth of a plant will not result in greater yields in any way. An experienced grower, who has seen the marijuana plant go through multiple life cycles over and over again, is always in better position to take that call. Some growers suggest that defoliation should be started in the vegetative stage itself. The idea is to create a more compact plant with more sites for buds to come out of.

A grower can make out it is time for a defoliation or "de-leafing" when there are more leaves than buds. It usually takes a week to 10 days for a plant start growing leaves again to the point that there are 4-5 leaves that have flattened and green enough to be ready to "de-leaf" again. Leaf removal stimulates growth of lower and mid-level buds by exposing them to direct high intensity which is generally reserved for the top level leaves otherwise.

Before plucking:

Photo Courtesy: growweedeasy.com

Immediately After Plucking:

Photo Courtesy: growweedeasy.com

Just four days later, look at the incredible bud growth:

Photo Courtesy: growweedeasy.com

Only Four Days After That (after another defoliation session):

Photo Courtesy: growweedeasy.com

Chapter 3: Using Nutrients

Photo Courtesy: growweedeasy.com

Like human beings, all plants and trees require nutrients to grow. But the trick is in finding the right nutrient that suits the plant and then using the appropriate amount of that nutrient to get the right result. Lower level of nutrients given regularly is better than putting a whole lot of nutrients together when growing marijuana.

Most nutrient bottles have 3 numbers inscribed on them, called N-P-K which stands for Nitrogen-Phosphorus-Potassium. A marijuana plant needs these 3 nutrients to grow depending on which stage of the life cycle they are in. For example, plants that are in a vegetative state currently need more nitrogen which powers the growth of leaves. However, in the flowering stages, a marijuana plant needs more phosphorus and less nitrogen to ensure better growth of the buds.

Because of the varied needs of the marijuana plant, it is easier for growers to use a professional nutrient system made specifically for a marijuana plant instead of trying to mix up one by themselves. With a professional nutrient system, a grower does not have keep track of the changing nutrient ratios at various stages of the plant growth. Risks of playing around with different types of nutrients incorrectly are also quite high.

A professional nutrient system saves a lot of time and energy of the grower. It is advisable to stay away from nutrients that claim to be "slow release" because they have been known to cause a lot of problems. The growing medium of the marijuana plant determines which nutrients need to be used where. If the plant is being grown on soil, nutrients made for soil would be required whereas if the plant is being grown in another medium like air or coco coir, nutrients made for hydroponics need to be used. Some nutrients like Canna Coco are available which were formulated to work best for growing marijuana in Coco Coir.

It is recommended to start at half-strength with new nutrients. If the grow lights are bright enough and the plants are growing fast, the strength of the nutrients can be increased. Plant use light as food to grow and not nutrients and just like humans, a marijuana plant cannot be subjected to heavy dosage of nutrients without any reason. It will result in yellowing of the plant which signifies nutrient burn.

Some growers believe it is necessary to push the nutrients to the plant. These growers keep increasing the dose of nutrients and look for signs of nutrient burn. But some growers think that as long as the plant is growing normally at the right speed, the nutrient is doing as much good as it can do and there is no need to increase the dosage. There are also some specific strains that require high level of nutrients.

One of the simplest and inexpensive nutrient systems that works great is **Dyna-Gro** – which constitutes of **Foliage-Pro and Bloom**. Dyna-Gro can be used to grow marijuana in air, soil, coco coir or any other medium. Dyna-Gro works well from seed to harvest and does not require the plant to have any additional nutrients. They do not build up salt in the soil and do not clog the hydroponic system. Some growers have even rated it higher than Advanced Nutrients which surprised many people as Advanced Nutrients have long been considered one of the best.

But just getting the correct nutrient and working out a schedule is not the only step that a grower should take. As a grower, it is important to know what effect the nutrients are having on the plant. Using too much nutrient results in "Nutrient Burn" – a sign of which is the yellowing of the tips of the leaves. Nutrients are like helpers which provide the plant with whatever it needs to carry out the process of photosynthesis and growth.

When growing in soil, one of the best things that a grower can do is to compost their own **super soil**. This can be made organically and will provide the marijuana plant with all the nutrients that are needed throughout the growth of the plant. Doing so will take the focus away from nutrients and deficiencies and instead focus the time and effort to maintain and train the plants.

Making Super Soil

A tried and tested method for creating super soil is illustrated below.

The following things would be needed:

Huge mixing container (enough to hold ~110 pounds of soil)
Rake
Tarp or large trash cans to hold soil while it's "cooking"

Ingredients required:

6 bags x 10-gallon (35 pounds or 1.5 cu. ft.) <u>Roots Organic Soil</u>
2 bags x 50L (35 lbs.) <u>Biobizz Light-Mix soil</u>

2 bags x 30 lbs. Organic Earthworm Castings

1 box 6 lbs. Fish Bone Meal (3-16-0)

1 cup Dolomite Lime

½ cup Azomite (0-0-0.2)

1 box 5 lbs. Blood Meal (12-0-0)

1 bag 4 lbs. Happy Frog Bat Guano (0-5-0)

¾ cup Epsom Salt

Once all the ingredients and tools are ready, the following steps need to be followed:

Mixing the soil

1. Of the 4 bags of Roots Organic Soil that are available, add 2 bags to the mixing area.

Photo Courtesy: growweedeasy.com

2. The Fish Bone meal needs to be added next

Photo Courtesy: growweedeasy.com

4. One bag of Biobizz to be added

Photo Courtesy: growweedeasy.com

5. Dolomite Lime and Granular Azomite to be sprinkled all over the pile

Photo Courtesy: growweedeasy.com

6. Last bag of Biobizz light mix to be added

Photo Courtesy: growweedeasy.com

7. First bag of worm castings to be added

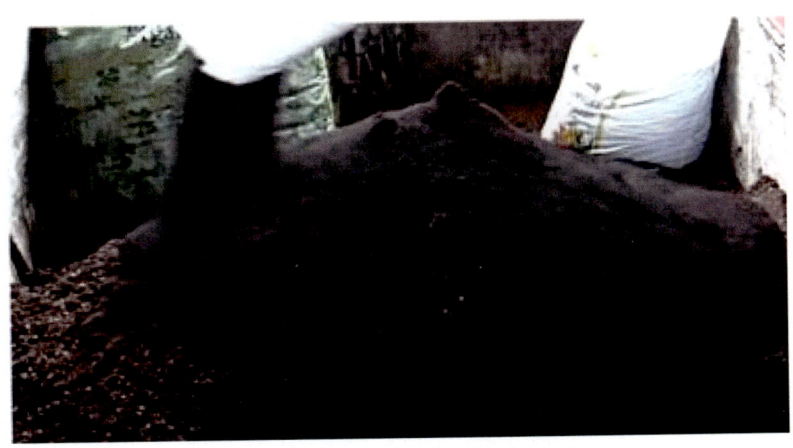

Photo Courtesy: growweedeasy.com

8. Another bag of the 2 left over Roots organic soil to be added thereafter

Photo Courtesy: growweedeasy.com

9. Mix the whole pile using a rake

Photo Courtesy: growweedeasy.com

10. 2nd bag of Worm Castings to be added

Photo Courtesy: growweedeasy.com

11. The last remaining bag of Roots Organic Soil to be added

Photo Courtesy: growweedeasy.com

12. Blood meal to be added next along with Bat Guano and Epsom Salt after which the whole mixture is to be raked thoroughly.

Photo Courtesy: growweedeasy.com

After the soil mixture has been prepared, the next step is Composting the soil.

Composting the Soil

1. A week or so is required for the soil to mix properly. A grower should continually keep mixing the soil to see that there are no color spots left.

2. The whole mixture needs to be transferred into closed containers for the next part of the

process. A few large garbage cans usually do the job very well.

3. After the mix has been transferred into a garbage can, a little water is to be added to the mix to start the microbial process. The mixture can be moist but not soggy. The reason that this mixture is being put in closed containers is that otherwise the mixture will dry out completely if kept in open containers. This will stop the microbial process and will not help in making good quality soil.

4. After adding water, the containers or garbage cans should be placed in a sunny place and allowed to "cook" for around 60 days. During this time, the moisture content of the soil needs to maintained and the containers should always be kept closed. This will trap the heat inside the container and together with the microbial process make the soil heat up. Growers need not be alarmed by this. What happens during this "cooking" is that all the ingredients that were put into the soil fuse together into a form that will be easy for the plant to ingest.

Some growers also suggest adding live worms to this mix to aerate the soil even more. The worms cause no harm to the marijuana plant and can be used when planting the plants in a pot as well.

5. Before moving on to the next stage of "Growing," the soil needs to mixed one last time.

Start Growing

Once the Super Soil mixture is ready, it is time to put them into containers or growing pots.

1. First, at least 1/3rd of the growing container needs to be filled with the "cooked" Super Soil mixture.

2. The rest of the container needs to be filled with regular soil. Some good soils available in the market are Fox farms Happy Frog Soil and Roots Organic Soil. The top of the growing containers need to be filled with regular soil because when the seed is planted and it starts to

grow in its infancy, the plant does not have the ability to withstand such strong nutrients that are put in the Super Soil. Once the seeds start growing and developing roots, it eventually reaches the bottom portion of the container containing the Super Soil and by then the seed has grown into a plant with roots and can utilize the nutrients present in the soil.

3. Before planting the seeds, growers need to ensure that the seeds have germinated. Germination of seeds is the process of getting the marijuana seeds to sprout. The grower will realize that the seeds have germinated when they see a white tendril appear on the seed. This little tendril is the first root of the plant and is called a "taproot."

This taproot will then give life to more and more roots as the plants starts growing. Germination of seeds can be done using various easily available tools in the market like Rapid Rooters and Rockwool Cubes. Growers generally favor Rapid Rooters the most because it is the easiest to use and there are barely any chances to mess up when using them. After the marijuana seed has germinated, it is time to plant the seed in the growing pots. The seeds need to be planted in a way so that the white tendrils (taproot) face downwards. The top of the seed should ideally be just below the growing surface. It can take a couple of hours or a couple of days depending on the strain the grower is working with, before a young seedling can be seen emerging from the soil or any other growing medium that is being used by the grower. At this stage of the plant growth, it should be kept out of reach of bright lights. A marijuana plant needs light only when the first set of leaves start appearing. These first set of leaves are also known as "cotyledons."

4. After the seeds have been germinated and the first set of leaves start appearing, plenty of light and water needs to be provided to the plant. Once the plant is half the size that it is supposed to grow to eventually, it is advisable to change the light schedule to 12/12 (12 hours on and 12 hours off) till the flowering stage.

It is natural for plants to start losing leaves when it nears harvest as the plant puts all its energy into making buds. Some people see it as a call for increasing the level of nutrients, but doing so will only reduce the yield from the plant. Using too much nutrients, especially Nitrogen, suppresses the growth of buds properly. However, if the nutrient levels are kept low and the vegetative growth is allowed to die away during the last few weeks, the buds swell up dramatically compared to a plant which is kept green all the way to the harvest.

Keeping the nutrient level low as harvest approaches is also helpful in ensuring there is no taste of the nutrient on the buds which remained unutilized before harvest. Lowering overall nutrients and letting the leaves yellow and fall improves the bud yields and also improves the overall taste and smell of the buds.

Some growers also used extra sugar like blackstrap molasses towards the end of flowering to get the buds to fatten up. This is especially effective for users of soil. If the plant is grown in soil, an effective alternative to nutrients and other expensive supplements is a teaspoonful of blackstrap molasses added to the water every time a grower waters their plants.

Photo Courtesy: growweedeasy.com

Chapter 4: Temperature and Humidity Control

For the final potency and yield from a marijuana plant, a good growing environment is extremely crucial. If the temperature mainly, and the humidity to an extent, is too high or too low, the plant will not grow properly and produce fat and dense buds no matter what one does. Too high temperatures will also reduce the potency and smell by destroying the cannabinoids and terpenes.

Marijuana plants like a comfortable room temperature when growing indoors, maybe a little warmer but not too dry or too humid. If a grower feels too hot or too cold in the grow room, it is possible that the plant feels the same way as well. This might be a sign to change the temperature or humidity of the grow area. Generally marijuana plants prefer a temperature ranging from 70 degrees Fahrenheit to 85 degrees Fahrenheit.

Photo Courtesy: growweedeasy.com

During the vegetative stage, young growing marijuana plants prefer temperatures warmer than the flowering stage in the range of 70 degrees Fahrenheit to 85 degrees Fahrenheit. But in the flowering stage, it is best to keep the temperature slightly cooler – in the range of 65 degrees Fahrenheit to 80 degrees Fahrenheit to produce the best color and smell. It is advisable to keep a difference of 10 degrees between night and day temperatures especially during the flowering stage for best quality buds. Cold temperatures slow down the growth of the marijuana plant and too low temperatures may even kill a plant. The plant is also susceptible to certain molds when the temperature is too low. Frequent temperature changes lead to over purpling of leaves and can also reduce photosynthesis. In the same way, if the temperature in the grow area is too high; it may kill the plant or slow down the growth of the plant. Temperatures above 80 degrees Fahrenheit in the flowering stage are sure to make the buds of the marijuana plant less potent and will reduce the smell from the buds. Heat also makes a marijuana plant susceptible to other problems like spider mites, white powdery mildew, root rot, nutrient burn etc.

The color of the leaves and buds are also determined by the temperature that a marijuana plant experiences. Temperature fluctuation can change how a plant grows. A marijuana plant prefers a cool temperature at night and slightly cooler temperatures will encourage growth but if the temperature is even slightly higher, the growth of the plant will be impeded. However, it is possible to use these characteristics to train the plant. If the plant grows too long and there is requirement to slow down the growth of the plants, increasing the temperature at night will help.

Temperature and relative humidity are closely related and sometimes it is possible to eliminate issues with one by working on the other. "Humidity" in general means the amount of water that is being currently help in the air in the grow area while "Relative Humidity" compares that amount to the amount of water that can be held at that temperature in the grow room. Plants can survive and grow at different levels of relative humidity in the air. If the humidity in the air is too high, dew starts forming on the leaves of the plant, which leads to formation of molds. Greenhouse growers sue the term VPD – Vapor Pressure Deficit – to measure the temperature and relative humidity. If the air is hot and dry i.e. high VPD, the plant will have a slow growth. And when the air is cold and humid i.e. low VPD, the plants will grow slowly and lead to formation of molds/fungus. Both temperature and relative humidity needs to be controlled to get the best yields from your marijuana plant.

Optimal Temperature at Different Stages

Clones

Clones prefer slightly warmer than room temperature with high humidity. Temperature should ideally be between 70 degree Fahrenheit and 80 degree Fahrenheit. Since clones do not have a root system yet, all their water related needs have to be fulfilled by the transpiration of the leaves. Some growers use humidity domes to artificially raise the humidity for clones.

Photo Courtesy: growweedeasy.com

Seedling or Vegetative Stage

At this stage, the plant prefers room temperature or slightly warmer temperatures with low humidity. A young seedling grows faster with high temperature and humidity but as the plant gets older, a low temperature and low humidity does not affect it much. A marijuana plants ability to withstand colder temperatures and low humidity increases at its age increases. Keeping the temperature between 70-80 degrees Fahrenheit is ideal in this stage during the day and slightly low temperatures during the night. Cooler night temperatures promote fast and healthy growth.

Flowering Stage

In the flowering stage, it is preferable to avoid hot temperatures and keep the humidity levels low with slightly cooler temperatures at night. Unless the plant is being supplemented with additional CO_2, temperatures should be kept under 80 degrees Fahrenheit. Higher temperatures during the flowering stage cannot only cause an issue for the growth of buds, it will also affect the terpenes and cause them to evaporate into the air. And burning away the tarpenes will impact the taste and smell of the buds adversely.

It is advisable to give the plant colder temperatures at night, especially towards the end of the flowering stage to increase the tarpene content and production of trichome in the buds of the plant.

Chapter 5: Drying and Curing Buds

Photo Courtesy: growweedeasy.com

Even though good genetics and growing a plant properly are important for producing top quality buds, the job of the grower does not finish with the cutting down of the plants during harvest. How a grower dries and cures the buds amounts to about 50% of the final bud quality. To cure the marijuana buds perfectly a grower needs wide mouthed mason jars and a drying rack. If a drying track is not available, a sieve or a mesh over a round utensil can also serve the purpose. Thereafter, the following steps need to be followed to cure the marijuana perfectly:

1. Cutting the plant – A grower can either cut out the branches or the whole plant before readying them for drying. In areas of less humidity, buds maybe left on the branches to slow down the process of drying.

2. Trimming – Extra fan leaves on the buds need to trimmed away. This will not only make the bud look better, it will also make the buds smoother. Leaving leaves behind will make the buds harsher.

Trimming Your Buds

3. Slow Drying – Hanging buds upside down is the most standard way of drying them. But it is important to dry them slowly because drying up the

buds too fast takes away the smell and effect of the buds. A grower can use simple hangers and clips to dry the buds.

4. Continuing to dry the buds for another 3-7 days – If buds dry up in 3-4 days, it has probably dried up too soon. If all the moisture is removed from the buds, the curing process will slow down dramatically. Over dried buds will cure too, but it will take a long time.

5. Placing the buds in jars – Once the buds have been cured, they can be placed in mason jars. Once the buds have been put in jars, for the first 1-2 weeks, the jars need to be opened and the grower needs to let it air out to continue the curing process. The buds will continue to cure for up to 6 months. After the buds have cured completely, they should ideally be placed in vacuum-sealed packs.

Step-by-Step guide to control temperature in the grow room

1. **Get a thermometer** – Digital thermometers which display both temperature and humidity are easily available in the market and it is one of the

first tools that are required before a grower starts planting the seeds.

2. **Refer to the temperature chart** – Refer to the temperature chart below to ensure that the temperature of the grow room is not too high or too low.

Vegetative Stage: 70-85°F (20-30°C)
Flowering Stage: 65-80°F (18-26°C)
Photo Courtesy: growweedeasy.com

3. **Adjust temperature if it is too high or too low** – There are many tools to help control the temperature in a grow room but growers struggling

with both hot and cold temperatures in the place they live can consider getting an All-In-One Heater and Air Conditioner.

Steps to take:

1. Exhaust system: It is important to have a good exhaust system in place to suck out the hot air and keep the air circulation going in a grow area. Exhaust should be connected to the hot grow lights, so that the hot air can be pulled outside.

Photo Courtesy: growweedeasy.com

2. Air Circulation: If the air circulation in your grow area is poor, hot spots will tend to develop

in the grow area which will damage the plants. It is a good idea to have small fans installed all over the grow area so that the air keeps circulating and does not focus of any one area particularly.

3. <u>Changing the light schedule:</u> A grower can change ones light schedule so that the grow lights are turned off at certain parts of the day when the temperature is too high, if they feel that the temperature is getting too high. For e.g. a plant requires at least 18 hours of light every day to grow properly. So a timer could be set which would switch the lights off for the stipulated 6 hours as desired.

4. <u>Changing the lights:</u> If the temperature of the grow area seems to be too high, there could be chance that the cause for that is that the installed grow lights are too bright. The lights can be moved further away from the plants to let the heat dissipate evenly or the light can be changed to a watt so that heat is not too much. Inversely, if the temperature seems too low, the light can be brought closer to the plant or a

higher watt light would be required to be bought.

5. <u>Other ways:</u> There are other ways of altering the temperature of the grow area by using appliances like Air Conditioner or Air Cooler or a Heater. It is also possible to insulate the grow area by using rolls of insulating materials that are available easily. Insulating the grow area will keep the heat inside the grow area when the temperature outside is too cold.

Chapter 6: Timing the Harvest

For most strains of marijuana, the window for harvest is a period of around 2-3 weeks. If a grower harvests the plant before harvest, the yield from the plant will be very low. It is advisable to allow the buds to ripen fully before starting harvest. In the last 2-3 weeks, the buds have been recorded to grow over 25%. For impatient growers harvesting the plant is as important as growing it. Harvesting ahead of time will lead to low potency and yields and waiting too long will turn the buds into a batch of sleeping medicine. A grower needs three things to determine the best time for harvesting:

1. The knowledge to identify the time of harvest
2. Visual inspection
3. A magnifying tool

When it comes to magnifying tools, some of the tools that are widely used by growers all over the world are:

- Jewelers Loupe – It is the cheapest and most basic way to check the plants if they are ready for harvest, but they are not the most reliable.

- Handheld Magnifier – These can magnify to a far greater extent than a jewelers loupe but it is harder to focus using these.
- Digital Microscope – This is the most expensive of all the options but is totally worth the money spent on it. It gives the closest details and required a laptop to be connected.

There are two ways of identifying the right time to harvest the marijuana plant:

1. **'The Pistil Method'**

    Pistils refer to the hair on the buds on the marijuana plant. The idea is to check the pistils to see if they are still white or if they have darkened.

    Not ready to harvest

    In the picture below the pistils are white and still straight so they are absolutely too early to be harvested.

Photo Courtesy: growweedeasy.com

Still not ready to harvest

We need to wait till at least 40-50% of the pistils turn dark and look mature enough. In the picture below, the pistils have become darker but they still less than 40% curled/darkened pistils. This means there are still several weeks to go before they reach the highest levels of potency.

Photo Courtesy: growweedeasy.com

Ready for harvest pictures

When about 50-70% of the pistils have darkened and curled, the potency of the plant has reached its optimum level. For a more calming and relaxing effect, it is advisable to wait till 70-90% of the pistils have darkened.

Photo Courtesy: growweedeasy.com

Different strains look different at the time of harvest and with some strains of marijuana, it is much harder to know when the right time to harvest is. Talking to the breeder of that particular strain will be helpful to growers who are growing a particular strain for the first time.

2. 'Trichome Method'

The Trichome method is a more accurate method of determining if the plant is ready for harvest than the Pistils Method described earlier.

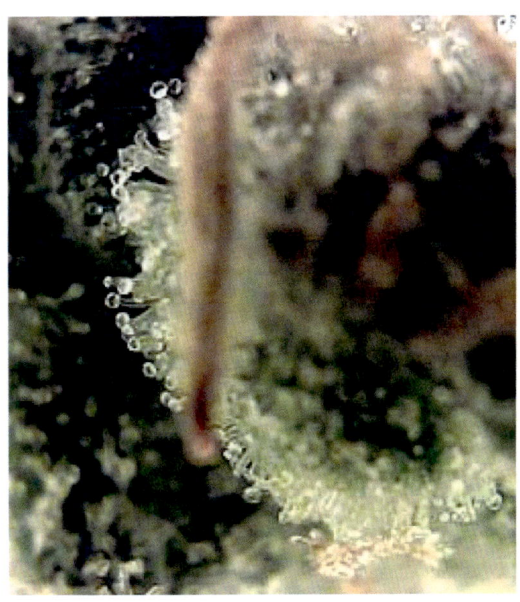

Photo Courtesy: growweedeasy.com

With this method a grower needs to look at the glandular stalked trichomes on the buds under a microscope. Trichomes make the marijuana so popular because of the way it looks – like mushrooms. In some parts, it is also known as 'raisin glands' or 'crystals' that accumulate on the buds or on the leaves of the marijuana plant. On looking under a microscope, there are other mushroom-like hairs on the buds but do not have a "mushroom head." These are not essential in determining the potency of the marijuana and hence need not be paid much importance. Trichomes which look like mushrooms with a ball-like top are the ones that contribute towards the potency of the marijuana. Using a digital microscope is the best way to detect if the plant is ready to be harvested.

Photo Courtesy: growweedeasy.com

Tips and Hints

1. If the white mushroom-like hairs on the buds are straight and still translucent, then the plant is still too young to be harvested.

2. The beginning of the harvest period is indicated when the trichomes have curled up slightly and at least 40% of the white hair has darkened.

3. The highest potency of the plant is reached when the trichomes become completely milky when viewed under a microscope. This leads to a more euphoric and psychoactive effect.

4. The end of the harvest window is indicated when the trichomes become darker almost amber/gold. These plants have a more relaxing effect because most of the trichomes have converted from THC to CBN. In some strains, the trichomes may even turn purple.

5. When the trichomes become gray and look dull and withered, it generally means that the harvesting window has already passed. The

buds from these plants will have an effect of putting the smoker to sleep without many psychoactive effects.

Conclusion

To conclude, there are various ways of increasing the yield from a marijuana plant, but the most basic of those is the lighting in a grow area. No matter how good the strain of marijuana is, it is next to impossible to have good yields if there isn't appropriate lighting. There is also a trick to make the plant use more lighting – to increase the level of CO_2 in the air in the grow area. However, if the plant is already taking in as much light as it possibly can, there are chances of the plant getting damaged. So adding CO_2 has potential risks and should be employed only if a grower thinks that the marijuana plant is not growing properly.

There are also methods to manipulate how the plant grows that gives a chance to increase the yield of the plant. The idea behind all these methods is to make sure that the light reaches to the mid and low level leaves and the plants do not grow tall but rather small and spread out like a bush instead of tree.

Using nutrients are also one of the methods to increase yield from a plant, but there are risks involved with this method too. If the nutrient supplied to the plant is in excess of what the plant needs or is not the right nutrient for the particular stage of growth that the plant is in, there are chances of damaging the plant by causing "Nutrient Burn." This is generally signified by the yellowing of the leaves at the edges.

Like lighting, temperature and humidity of the grow space is very important for the growth of a marijuana plant and the yield that it eventually produces. There are various "grow lights" available in the market to choose from and the grower has to make the choice between LED/CFL and HID as per their desire and objective. Of all the methods, one is more important to new growers than the others – knowing the right time to harvest.

Even if a grower follows all the methods as prescribed in this book, there is a huge chance that the grower will end up harvesting the plant ahead of time. It has been recorded that pre-harvesting of plants may lead to a loss of over 25% of yield.

Having the right tool like a digital microscope to keep an eye on the development of trichomes is very important to understand the appropriate time of harvest. As and when a grower keeps growing more batches of the plant, the understanding of how a marijuana plant functions keeps unfolding. After a while, the growers start to rely on their guts to ensure that the plant grows properly and make sure that the plant produces proper yields.

Finally, if you enjoyed this book, then I'd like to ask you for a favor, would you be kind enough to leave a short review for this book on Amazon? It would really help me out.

Thank you And Happy Growing!

Made in the USA
Lexington, KY
31 January 2018